Reading STREET

Grade K

AF478875

Scott Foresman

Classroom Management Handbook for Differentiated Instruction Practice Stations

PEARSON

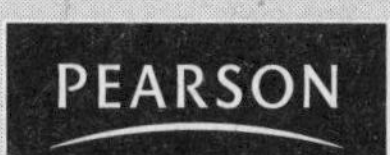

Glenview, Illinois • Boston, Massachusetts • Chandler, Arizona • Upper Saddle River, New Jersey

ISBN-13: 978-328-47766-1
ISBN-10:   328-47766-4
2 3 4 5 6 7 8 9 10 V0N4 14 13 12 11 10

Table of Contents

Welcome to Station Time!

Practice Stations Kit

The Leveled Practice Stations Kit helps simplify the task of managing stations by providing ideas for setting up classroom stations, weekly activities for each station, and suggested materials for each station.

Classroom Management Handbook for
Differentiated Instruction Practice Stations

The Management Handbook provides valuable resources to help you set up practice stations and to provide differentiated practice that enables you to address children at their instructional levels while they are working independently. The Scott Foresman Differentiated Instruction Practice Stations help children develop as independent thinkers who take responsibility for their own learning. The Handbook provides a suggested classroom floor plan that can be adjusted to fit the particular needs of your classroom. An overview for each station provides suggestions for setting up the stations and essential materials to include. The reproducible Work Plans list tasks that children will complete at each station and help children plan and track their assignments at each station.

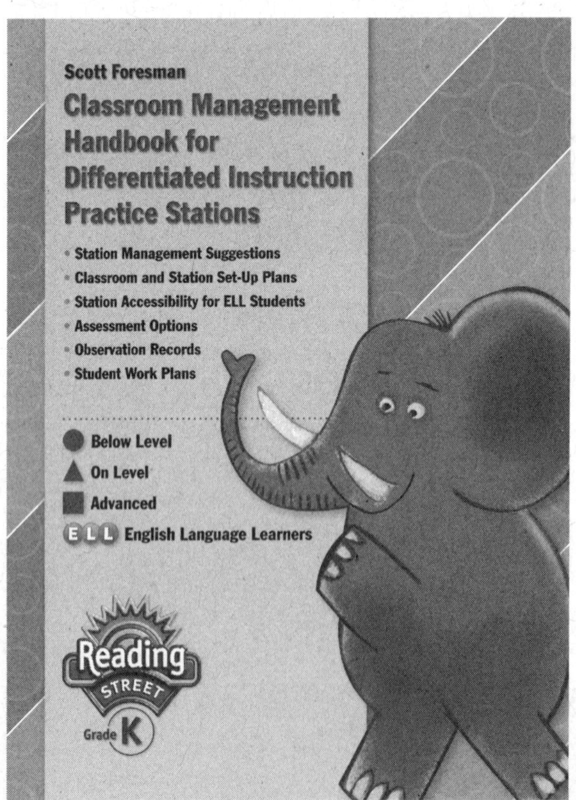

Practice Station Flip Charts

The Practice Stations Flip Charts are tabletop-sized flip charts with the Practice Stations activities from the Teacher's Edition. Each flip-chart page provides the weekly differentiated activities for that station. The activities provide opportunities for children to practice skills and to expand knowledge of the weekly concept. There are six flip charts, one for each station.

- Listen Up! (Phonemic Awareness Station)
- Word Work (Phonics Station)
- Words to Know (Vocabulary Station)
- Let's Write! (Writing Station)
- Read for Meaning (Comprehension Station)
- Let's Make Art! (Art Station)

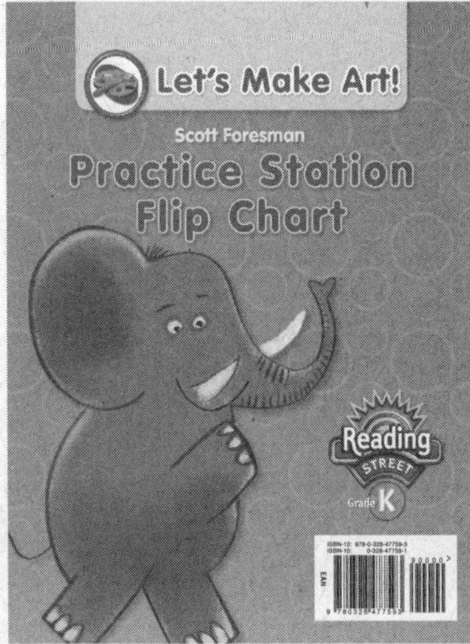

Setting Up the Stations

The classroom environment is an important factor in children's learning. To help create a comfortable environment that is conducive to learning, create separate spaces for the different types of instruction and activities that take place.

How can I set up the stations?

The thought of setting up stations in your classroom can be a bit daunting. This is especially true if you have a small classroom. Making room for stations can be accomplished if you start by thinking of the stations as extensions of your lessons.

- A station does not need to be large. A comfortable pillow in a cozy corner makes a great Read for Meaning station.

- With young children, pick a location for a station and maintain that location throughout the year.

- Set up your stations so that children will not distract those working independently or with you in a small group.

Productive Station Time

By taking time in the beginning to "teach" the station, your stations will enhance the learning in your room! Have fun with the stations; they are a powerful piece of your curriculum.

- Tell children what types of materials are in each station.

- Tell them what they will practice in each station. Explain the activity options provided in each station if they finish the assigned activity early.

- Model how to use the station and the materials in each station.

- Have children role play for the class appropriate behavior and possible situations they may encounter in the station.

- Explain how "My Work Plan" can help them keep track of the tasks they have completed.

- With young children it is often best to gradually add stations. Too much too soon is overwhelming!

TEACHER TiP

- Gather any material needed for next week's stations the week before. Have children organize the stations with materials needed and display the flip-chart page that explains the activity.

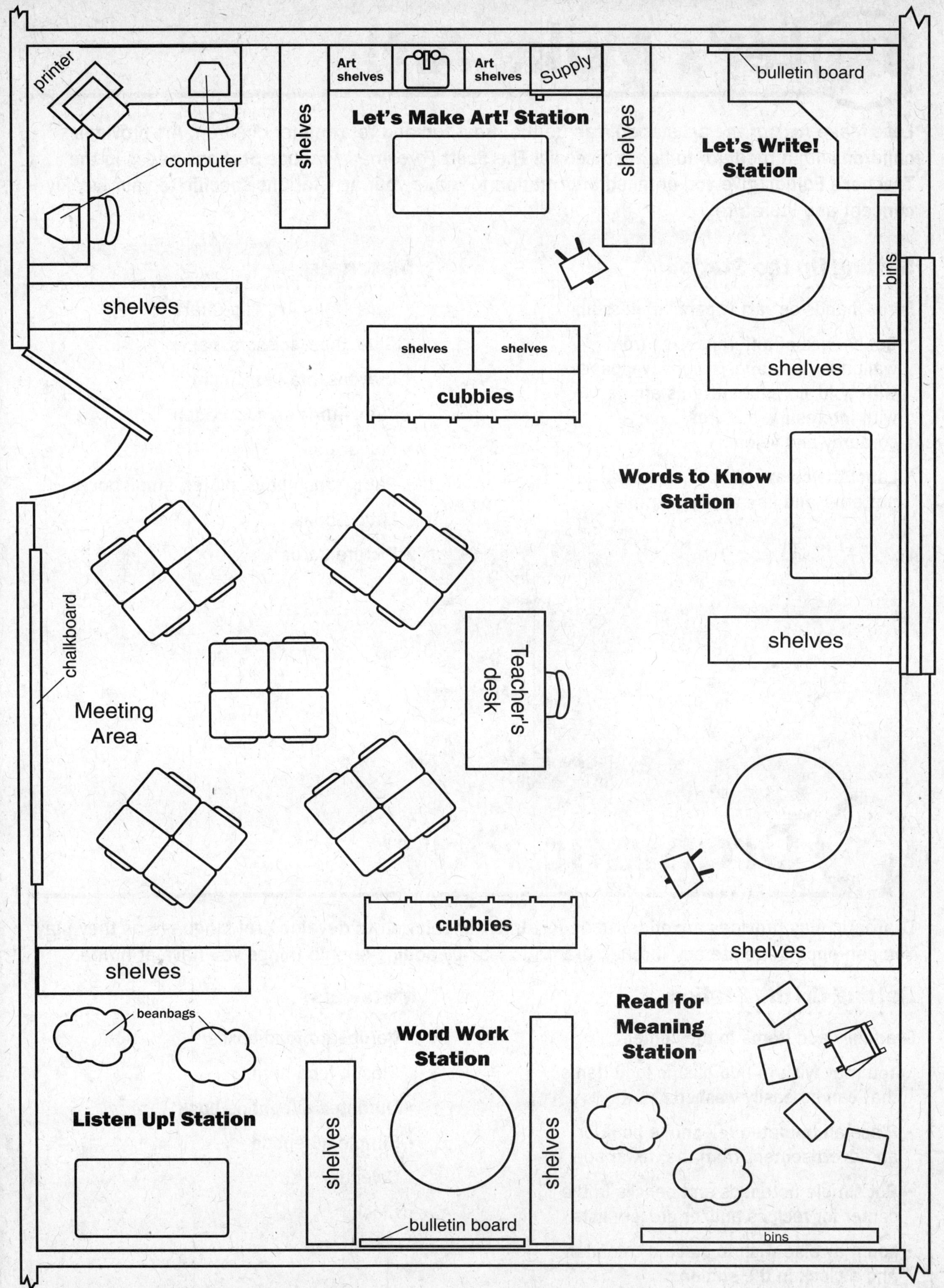

printer
computer
shelves
Art shelves
Art shelves
Supply
Let's Make Art! Station
shelves
bulletin board
Let's Write! Station
bins
shelves
shelves
cubbies
Words to Know Station
shelves
chalkboard
Meeting Area
Teacher's desk
cubbies
shelves
shelves
beanbags
Word Work Station
shelves
shelves
Read for Meaning Station
Listen Up! Station
bulletin board
bins

# Let's Make Art!

Let's Make Art!, or the art station, can be the most fun and relaxing for children. Art provides children with a medium to be themselves! The *Scott Foresman Practice Stations* pages in the Teacher's Edition give you detailed information to make your art stations specific to your weekly concept and literature.

Setting Up the Station

For a "hands-on" art vocabulary lesson:

- Cut shapes of different sizes from wallpaper or fabric. Choose wallpaper with bold, colorful patterns and fabric with interesting textures, such as corduroy and velour.

- Label the colors, shapes, textures, patterns, and lines in the samples.

Materials

- *Let's Make Art!* Flip Chart
- Glue, tape, scissors, paper
- Crayons, markers, paint
- Yarn, fabric scraps, cotton
- Magazines
- Paper lunch bags, plates, small boxes
- Little Books
- Picture Cards

# Dramatic Play

Dramatic play provides a wonderful opportunity for children to develop oral language as they play. You can encourage literacy through dramatic play by adding simple things you have at home.

Setting Up the Station

Gradually add items to the center.

- You may wish to add plastic food items that can be easily washed.

- Place an outdated telephone book or an advertisement from the newspaper.

- Put simple notepads and pencils in the center for recipes and/or grocery lists.

- You may also wish to place a calendar and a clock in the station.

Materials

- Cardboard food boxes
- Plastic food items
- Outdated telephone book
- Simple notepads
- Calendar
- Clock

Listen Up!

Listen Up! is the phonemic awareness station. For many teachers, setting up a phonemic awareness station is a challenge because children have a wide range of abilities. It is important to provide a variety of options to meet the needs of all children. At the phonemic awareness station, children listen for sounds as they say the name of the image on the Picture Cards and match those that rhyme or sort by initial, medial, or final sounds.

Setting Up the Station

Find a quiet space for this station where children will be able to hear letter sounds and words that rhyme.

- Picture Cards can be used at a table or on the floor. Include a table and chairs as well as carpet squares and beanbags in this area.

- Display pictures and objects that have names with a variety of letter sounds.

- Change the pictures and objects on occasion to provide new examples of letter sounds.

Materials

- *Listen Up!* Flip Chart
- Picture Cards
- Teacher-made word cards
- Paper, pencils, crayons
- Magazines, books, catalogs, maps, or other sources of colorful photos and art
- Objects that can be used to provide examples of letter sounds

Word Work

Setting up Word Work, the phonics station, presents another challenge because of the wide range of abilities among children. You need to have a variety of materials and options to meet the needs of all children.

Setting Up the Stations

The phonics station is where children can find letters on the Alphabet Cards or build words with Letter Tiles and then write the words on a word list.

As you review the work children do in the phonics station, look to see whether they are demonstrating an understanding of the phonics skills you have taught.

- Are they applying the target skill?
- Are they also applying previously learned skills to their work?

Materials

- *Word Work* Flip Chart
- Letter Tiles
- Magnetic Letters and Boards
- Alphabet Cards
- Picture Cards
- Teacher-made word cards
- Paper
- Pencils
- Crayons
- Blue and white index cards
- Decodable Practice Readers
- Write-On/Wipe-Off Boards
- Dictionaries and Pictionaries

Technology

- Letter Tile Drag and Drop
- Decodable eBooks

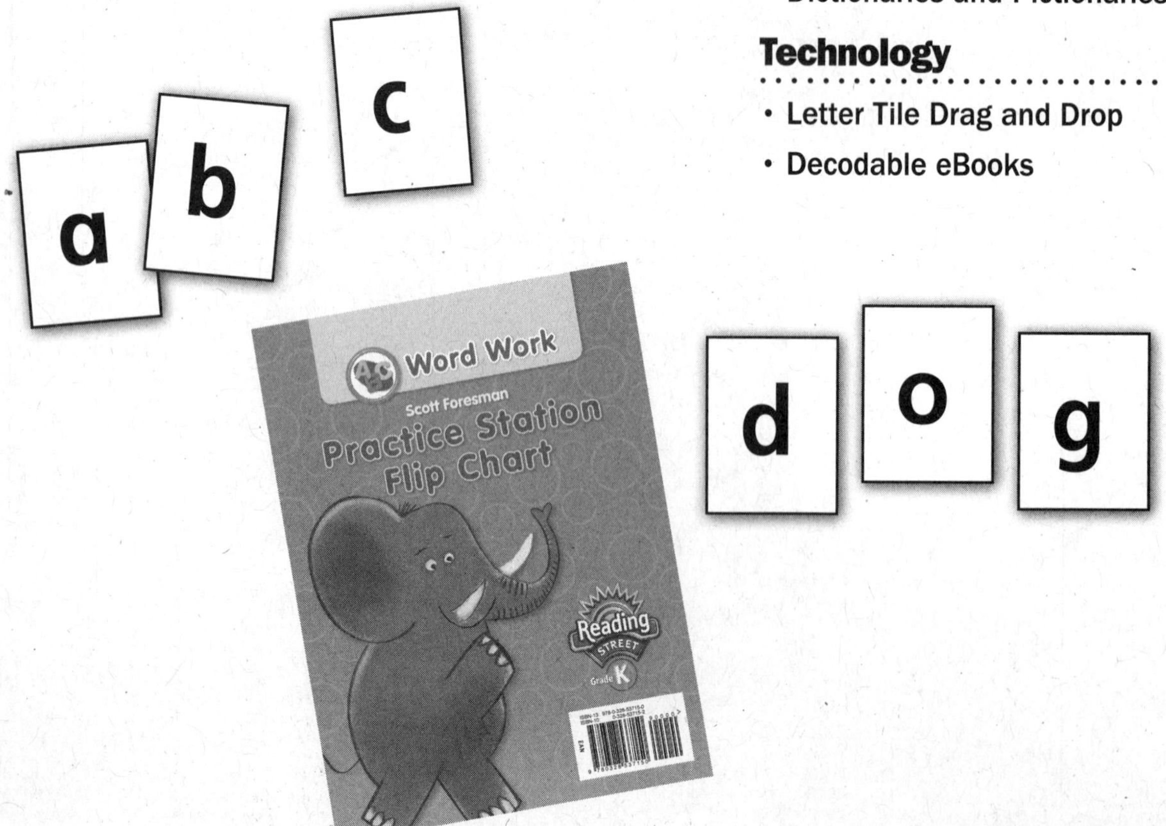

Words to Know

At Words to Know, the vocabulary station, children use various activities to practice and demonstrate their ability to identify and spell the lesson high-frequency words.

Setting Up the Station

- Supplement the station with other language-rich vocabulary-building activities.

- Post previously learned vocabulary in the station and encourage children to use these additional words when possible in speaking and writing.

Materials

- *Words to Know* Flip Chart
- Picture Cards
- Teacher-made word cards
- Paper, pencil, crayons
- Magazines, books, catalogs, maps, or other sources of colorful photos and art
- Objects that can be used to provide examples of the vocabulary words
- Dictionaries and Pictionaries

Technology

- Vocabulary Activities
- Journal Word Bank
- Amazing Words Sing with Me Animations

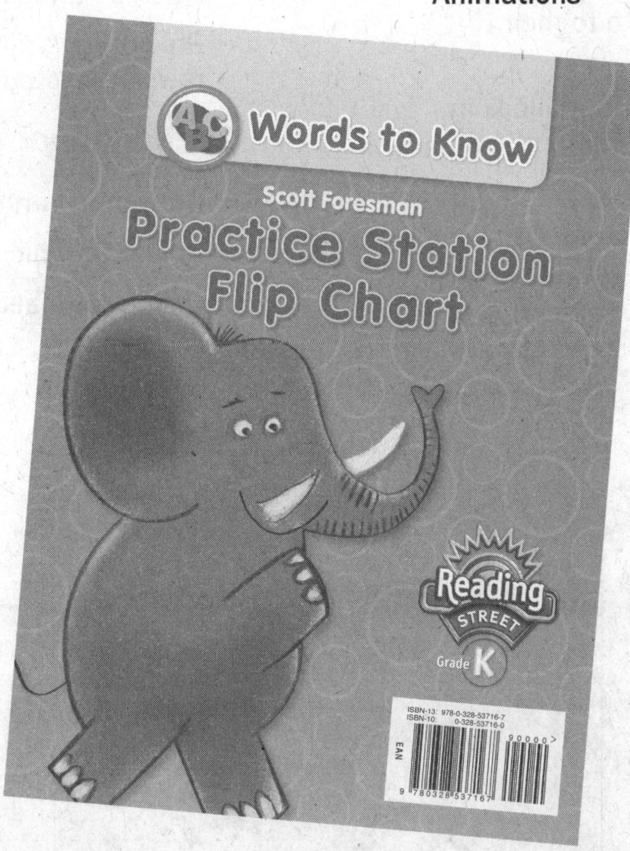

Let's Write!

The writing station is another place where you need to address a wide range of abilities. Children need to begin where they are. The more resources you provide in the station, the more successful it will be for all. As you review the work children do in the writing station, look to see whether they are applying the skill you have introduced. Writing is an excellent way to assess phonetic development.

Setting Up the Station

Let's Write! may need more space than other stations.

- Designate a table for children who are working on prewriting and drafting activities and another for revising, editing, and publishing.

- Set up computers for word processing on another table or on a group of desks.

- Write the Amazing Words and the high-frequency words for the week on index cards and place them in the station. Encourage children to write using Amazing Words and high-frequency words.

- Encourage children to write to their friends.

- Place envelopes and a class mailbox in the station; children can write and mail letters.

Materials

- *Let's Write!* Flip Chart
- Writing Steps poster
- Word Cards
- Poem Starters
- Little Books
- Copies of letter and invitation formats
- Picture Cards
- Pencils, markers, crayons, scissors, glue, glitter, yarn, hole punch
- Magazines, catalogs, or other sources of pictures that can be cut up
- Word banks, dictionaries, pictionaries, writer's handbooks
- Prewriting graphic organizers and revising and editing checklists

Technology

- Grammar Jammer
- Online Graphic Organizers
- Online Journals

Read for Meaning

At Read for Meaning, the reading comprehension station, children can read by themselves or with partners to practice and review the target comprehension skills and strategies. They can make connections across texts, explore personal interests, or find out more about topics, authors, and genres that are related to the weekly concept.

Setting Up the Station

Find a comfortable space for this station away from the main activity of the classroom.

- Include a table and chairs as well as rocking chairs, carpet squares, or beanbags.
- Use shelves, wire rack bins, or plastic tote trays to create an organized classroom library.
- Gradually add and take away books to avoid having too many books, which can overwhelm children.
- Group books by theme, topic, genre, reading level, or author.

Materials

- *Read for Meaning* Flip Chart
- Leveled Readers
- Decodable Practice Readers
- Ready, Set, Roll! Readers
- Little Books
- Books by topics and themes
- Books by favorite authors
- Class-made books
- Paper, pencils, crayons
- Magazines and other reference sources
- Graphic organizers

Technology

- Decodable eBooks
- Leveled Reader Database
- Reading Street Leveled Readers CD-ROM
- Envision It! Animations
- Online Graphic Organizers

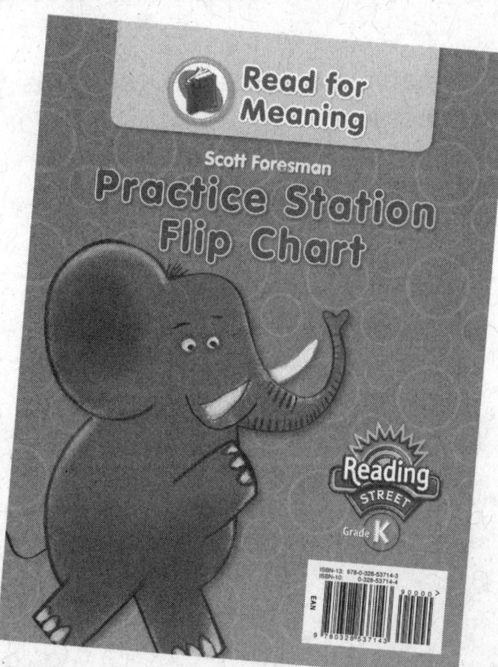

ELL-Accessible Stations

The *Scott Foresman Practice Stations* can be adapted to be more accessible to English language learners. Frontloading suggestions and background building information found in the core lesson help support all of the independent activities in the stations. Modeling with picture cues, real objects, and role-playing can help English language learners understand what they need to do without solely depending on language. Children should be encouraged to listen, speak, read, and write during their time in each station. Enhance language production by structuring cooperative learning opportunities at the Practice Stations. Pair children who share the same home language, or have more proficient children work with newcomers. This extra support provides a positive example and support for completing activities in the stations. The stations provide an environment where children can feel comfortable practicing English without worrying about errors they might make.

Listen Up! and Word Work

Listen Up! and Word Work, the phonemic awareness and phonics stations, practice a similar set of skills each week, so the stations can be adapted in similar ways. Encourage children to decode the words aloud with a partner. Use the following suggestions to adapt the phonemic awareness and phonics stations for English language learners.

- Be sure that children understand the meanings of all of the words before they use the station.

- When possible, introduce any cognates or language transfer skills that will help children better understand the words practiced.

- Review the words or patterns using the Sound-Spelling Charts.

- Use one of the Alphabet Cards to introduce the word.

- Write the word and point to the letters of the word as you say each sound. Model blending each word.

- Have groups of mixed abilities use Letter Tiles to match the words with the cards. Children should write each letter of the words. Offer guidance as necessary.

Words to Know

English language learners can benefit in Words to Know, the vocabulary station, by using visuals and real objects to scaffold meaning. Children should be encouraged to use their home languages to transfer any vocabulary knowledge or strategies to what they are practicing. The following suggestions can be used to adapt the vocabulary station.

- Introduce any cognates or language transfer skills that will help children better understand the lesson vocabulary.

- Use visuals and gestures to review the meaning of words.

- Revisit the words with children daily. Help children say each word aloud and encourage oral production throughout the day.

- Have groups of mixed abilities work together choosing Picture Cards. Have more advanced children match word cards and Picture Cards.

Let's Write!

Children at all proficiency levels should be given a variety of materials they need to be able to write successfully. Some children may benefit from brainstorming and using graphic organizers to plan their writing while some may benefit by working independently with a writing prompt. The suggested adaptations below may help your English language learners succeed in the writing station.

- Provide sentence frames, writing prompts, or writing models to assist children's writing.

- For beginning and intermediate children, write out sentences they dictate. Allow them to copy the sentences and then read them aloud to you. Children can also draw a picture and label the different parts.

- More advanced children can write a sentence and share with a partner.

Read for Meaning

Have a variety of Little Books and Concept Literacy Readers available at the comprehension station. Children may benefit from reviewing the comprehension skill with the Envision It! pictures in *My Skills Buddy*. The comprehension station may be adapted using the following suggestions.

- When possible, use picture cues to review the comprehension skill.

- Choose a passage or selection that is appropriate to children's reading level. Read aloud the text with the children.

- During reading, ask questions or fill out a graphic organizer with children to monitor their comprehension.

- Allow beginning and intermediate children to orally explain the relationships between the comprehension skill and the passage read. More advanced children can complete this activity by writing a sentence or drawing and labeling a picture.

Let's Make Art!

Art and dramatic play give children the opportunity to express themselves in a creative way. Children may benefit from seeing a completed art project before they begin theirs. Adapt the art station for English language learners using the following suggestions.

- Be sure children understand the art or dramatic play activity before they work individually or In small groups.

- Have groups of mixed-ability children work together in dramatic play. Encourage all children to participate equally.

- Give children time to plan their art projects before they begin and also allow them to explain their art project to a partner or to the class when they are finished.

The Practice Stations provide valuable opportunities for children to gain knowledge and increase their confidence, thereby making their social and academic classroom experiences more meaningful. In addition, children's involvement in the stations will strengthen their performance in all areas of instruction, and their work in the stations will positively affect their ability to function as active and independent learners.

Assessing Station Activities

Using Assessment to Guide Instruction Informal, ongoing assessments are important means of guiding classroom instruction, and station activities provide excellent opportunities for ongoing assessments.

Station time is an extension of your lesson. It provides an opportunity for you to work with small groups, but it is not "busy time" for the other children. Station time provides a wonderful opportunity for you to assess how well children can apply what you have taught. The work they do during station time is an important piece of your assessment of the whole child!

There are many formal and informal ways to assess children and their work. Many of these assessments include children assessing their own work. Use the activities throughout the school year to measure children's growth and development.

The following assessment tools may be helpful as you informally assess children's station work.

Rubrics

- Create simple pictorial rubrics to guide children in assessing their own work.

- Use a rubric to guide your assessment of children's creativity and motivation.

Portfolios

- Save work children complete during station time. Use portfolio contents to measure children's progress and growth over time.

Informal Observations

- You may want to use a notebook or the Observation Record on page 17 to record your observations of children.

- Divide the class into small groups. Focus on observing a small group of children during station time each day instead of trying to observe all children's behaviors.

- Determine ahead of time what you will observe each week. Perhaps it is social interactions or emotional development. Some weeks you may wish to focus on academic development. Determining your expectations will help narrow your assessment.

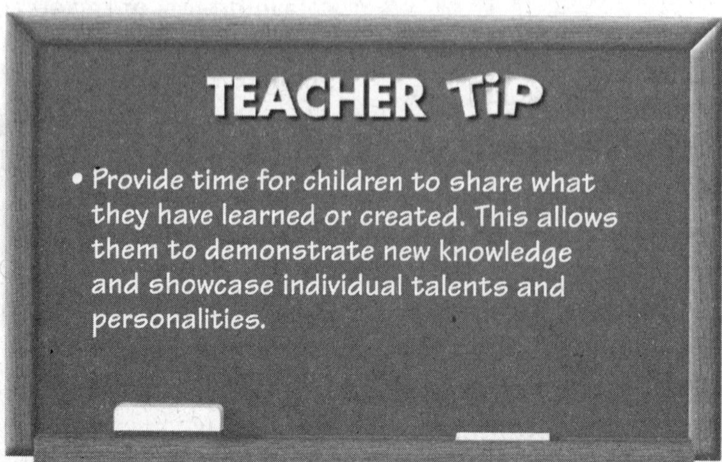

Observation Record

Date........................ Child..

Date........................ Child..

Date........................ Child..

Date........................ Child..

Date........................ Child..

Date........................ Child..

Student Work Plans

What Are Student Work Plans?

Pages 19–54 contain lesson-specific reproducible work plans for children to use during their independent activity time. Each work plan lists the tasks that children will complete, in stations or independently, while you meet with small groups. The work plans help children remember their assignments, plan their time, and keep track of what they've done. Work plans allow children to take responsibility and will aid them in becoming successful independent learners.

How Do I Use the Student Work Plans?

Begin by explaining the activities in the Practice Stations to children. Then distribute copies of *My Work Plan* and review the tasks. Be sure children understand that they will check the box next to each task as they complete it. Remind children that if they finish an activity before time is up, they should answer the Wrap Up Your Week questions or read silently. At the end of the week, you can collect children's work plans, or you can send them home.

If you prefer, you can customize a work plan for one or more children or for use during a particular lesson. For this purpose, a generic work plan can be found on p. 55.

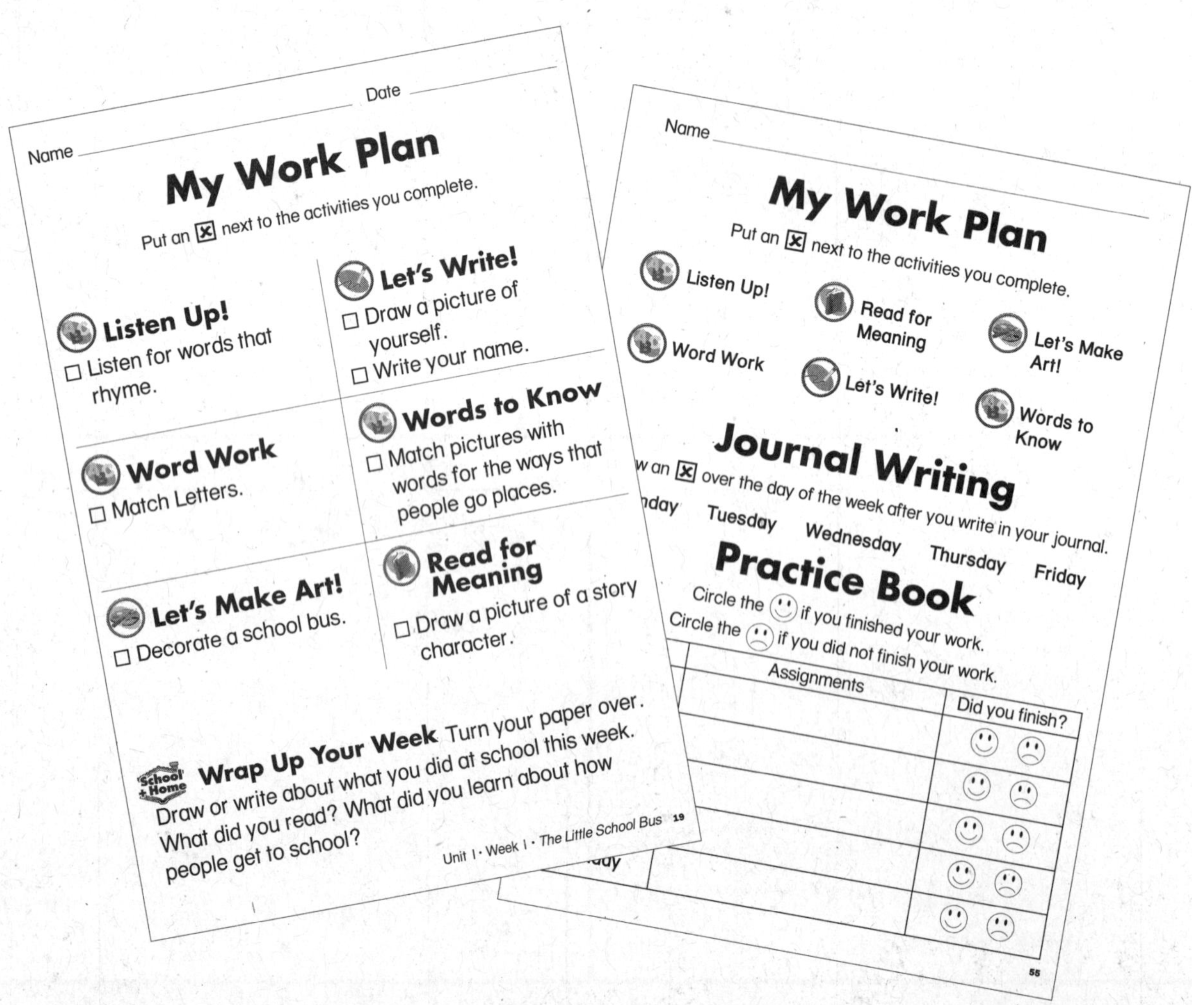

My Work Plan

Put an ☒ next to the activities you complete.

 ## Listen Up!

☐ Listen for words that rhyme.

 ## Let's Write!

☐ Draw a picture of yourself.
☐ Write your name.

 ## Word Work

☐ Match Letters.

 ## Words to Know

☐ Match pictures with words for the ways that people go places.

 ## Let's Make Art!

☐ Decorate a school bus.

 ## Read for Meaning

☐ Draw a picture of a story character.

Wrap Up Your Week Turn your paper over. Draw or write about what you did at school this week. What did you read? What did you learn about how people get to school?

My Work Plan

Put an ☒ next to the activities you complete.

 ## Listen Up!

☐ Listen for words that rhyme.

 ## Let's Write!

☐ Draw a picture of yourself.
☐ Write your name.

 ## Word Work

☐ Match Letters.

 ## Words to Know

☐ Match pictures with words for the ways that people go places.

 ## Let's Make Art!

☐ Decorate a school bus.

 ## Read for Meaning

☐ Draw a picture of a story character.

Wrap Up Your Week Turn your paper over. Draw or write about what you did at school this week. What did you read? What did you learn about helping others?

My Work Plan

Put an ☒ next to the activities you complete.

 ## Listen Up!

☐ Listen for word parts.

 ## Let's Write!

☐ Make an invitation.

 ## Word Work

☐ Match Letters.

 ## Words to Know

☐ Match pictures with words for colors.

 ## Let's Make Art!

☐ Paint a picture that shows how you work and play together at school.

 ## Read for Meaning

☐ Show where the story takes place.

School + Home **Wrap Up Your Week** Turn your paper over. Draw or write about what you did at school this week. What did you read? What did you learn about cooperating?

My Work Plan

Put an ☒ next to the activities you complete.

 ## Listen Up!

☐ Listen for and match sounds at the beginning of words.

 ## Let's Write!

☐ Finish a poem.

 ## Word Work

☐ Match Letters.

 ## Words to Know

☐ Match pictures with words for shapes.

 ## Let's Make Art!

☐ Make a collage that shows how people help each other.

 ## Read for Meaning

☐ Show what happens first, next, and last in the story.

School + Home **Wrap Up Your Week** Turn your paper over. Draw or write about what you did at school this week. What did you learn about community helpers?

My Work Plan

Put an ☒ next to the activities you complete.

 ## Listen Up!

☐ Listen for sounds at the beginning of words.

 ## Let's Write!

☐ Show the steps for watering a plant.

 ## Word Work

☐ Match Letters.

 ## Words to Know

☐ Match pictures with words for places.

 ## Let's Make Art!

☐ Paint a picture of someone in your school who helps you.

 ## Read for Meaning

☐ Group things that belong together.

Wrap Up Your Week Turn your paper over. Draw or write about what you did at school this week. What did you read? What did you learn about animals and people working and playing together.

My Work Plan

Put an ☒ next to the activities you complete.

 ## Listen Up!

☐ Find objects with names that begin with the same sound as in *mop*.

 ## Let's Write!

☐ Write a caption.

 ## Word Work

☐ Find things with names that begin with the letter *Mm*.

 ## Words to Know

☐ Find pictures that show *in, out, up,* or *down*.

 ## Let's Make Art!

☐ Use shapes to make a machine that helps people.

 ## Read for Meaning

☐ Name and tell about a character in a story.

School + Home **Wrap Up Your Week** Turn your paper over. Draw or write about what you did at school this week. What did you read? What did you learn about machines?

My Work Plan

Put an ☒ next to the activities you complete.

 ## Listen Up!

☐ Find objects with names that being with the same sound as *tiger*.

 ## Let's Write!

☐ Draw and write about how you help your friends.

 ## Word Work

☐ Find things with names that begin or end with *Tt*.

 ## Words to Know

☐ Match pictures with words for sizes.

 ## Let's Make Art!

☐ Draw a picture of a machine that helps people.

 ## Read for Meaning

☐ Group things that belong together.

Wrap Up Your Week Turn your paper over. Draw or write about what you did at school this week. What did you read? What did you learn about flowers?

My Work Plan

Put an ☒ next to the activities you complete.

 ## Listen Up!

☐ Find objects with the same beginning sound as in *apple* and middle sound as in *cat*.

 ## Let's Write!

☐ Write labels.

 ## Word Work

☐ Find things that have short *Aa* at the beginning or in the middle of its name.

 ## Words to Know

☐ Match pictures with words for colors.

 ## Let's Make Art!

☐ Make a flower.

 ## Read for Meaning

☐ Find things that are alike and different.

Wrap Up Your Week Turn your paper over. Draw or write about what you did at school this week. What did you read? What did you learn about nature?

My Work Plan

Put an ☒ next to the activities you complete.

 ## Listen Up!

☐ Find objects with the same beginning sound as in *sun* and end sound as in *bus*.

 ## Let's Write!

☐ Write a list.

 ## Word Work

☐ Find things that have *Ss* at the beginning or end of its name.

 ## Words to Know

☐ Match pictures with words for things in nature.

 ## Let's Make Art!

☐ Paint a picture of an animal in nature.

 ## Read for Meaning

☐ Show where the story takes place.

Wrap Up Your Week

Turn your paper over. Draw or write about what you did at school this week. What did you read? What did you learn about who lives in grasslands?

My Work Plan

Put an ☒ next to the activities you complete.

 ## Listen Up!

☐ Find objects with the same beginning sound as in *pig* and end sound as in *cup*.

 ## Let's Write!

☐ Write notes about what you read.

 ## Word Work

☐ Find things that have *Pp* at the beginning or end of its name.

 ## Words to Know

☐ Match pictures with words for animal babies.

 ## Let's Make Art!

☐ Draw a picture of a grasslands animal.

 ## Read for Meaning

☐ Find and tell what the book is mostly about.

School + Home **Wrap Up Your Week** Turn your paper over. Draw or write about what you did at school this week. What did you read? What did you learn about where bears hibernate?

My Work Plan

Put an ☒ next to the activities you complete.

Listen Up!

☐ Find objects with the same beginning sound as in *cat* and the end sound as in *duck*.

Let's Write!

☐ Write a poem about nature.

Word Work

☐ Find things with names that begin with the letter *Cc* as in *cat*.

Words to Know

☐ Match pictures with words for the seasons.

Let's Make Art!

☐ Draw a picture showing what happens in a story.

Read for Meaning

☐ Find pictures in a story that show what is real and make-believe.

School + Home **Wrap Up Your Week** Turn your paper over. Draw or write about what you did at school this week. What did you read? What did you learn about mouse's house?

My Work Plan

Put an ☒ next to the activities you complete.

 ## Listen Up!

☐ Find objects with the same beginning sound as in *inch* and middle sound as in *kitten*.

 ## Let's Write!

☐ Write a caption for a picture.

 ## Word Work

☐ Find objects that have short *Ii* at the beginning or in the middle of its name.

 ## Words to Know

☐ Order pictures to show what happens first, second, next, and last.

 ## Let's Make Art!

☐ Use shapes to make an animal's home.

 ## Read for Meaning

☐ Retell what happened first, next, and last in a story.

Wrap Up Your Week

Turn your paper over. Draw or write about what you did at school this week. What did you read? What did you learn about plants?

My Work Plan

Put an ☒ next to the activities you complete.

 ## Listen Up!

☐ Find objects that have the same middle sounds as *pig*.

 ## Let's Write!

☐ Write a story.

 ## Word Work

☐ Find objects what have short *Ii* at the beginning or in the middle of its name.

 ## Words to Know

☐ Find and use *left* and *right*.

 ## Let's Make Art!

☐ Make a poster about your favorite story.

 ## Read for Meaning

☐ Find pictures to show what is real and make-believe.

Wrap Up Your Week

Turn your paper over. Draw or write about what you did at school this week. What did you read? What did you learn about pandas?

My Work Plan

Put an ☒ next to the activities you complete.

 ## Listen Up!

☐ Find objects with names that begin with the same sounds as in *boat* and *nest*.

 ## Let's Write!

☐ Write a summary.

 ## Word Work

☐ Find objects with names that being with *Bb.*

 ## Words to Know

☐ Match pictures with words for color.

 ## Let's Make Art!

☐ Draw a picture to show how a panda changes as it grows.

 ## Read for Meaning

☐ Tell how things are alike or different.

School + Home **Wrap Up Your Week** Turn your paper over. Draw or write about what you did at school this week. What did you read? What did you learn about what you can do as you grow?

My Work Plan

Put an ☒ next to the activities you complete.

 ## Listen Up!
☐ Find objects with names that begin with the same sound as in *rug.*

 ## Let's Write!
☐ Write an invitation.

 ## Word Work
☐ Find objects with names that being with *Rr.*

 ## Words to Know
☐ Match words with pictures.

 ## Let's Make Art!
☐ Paint pictures to show what you can do as you grow and change.

 ## Read for Meaning
☐ Tell what happens at the beginning, middle, and end of a story.

School + Home **Wrap Up Your Week** Turn your paper over. Draw or write about what you did at school this week. What did you read? What did you learn about how people's lives have changed?

My Work Plan

Put an **X** next to the activities you complete.

 ## Listen Up!

☐ Find things with names that being with the same sounds as in *dog* and *cat*.

 ## Let's Write!

☐ Write a sentence to get others to agree with you.

 ## Word Work

☐ Find objects with names that begin with *Dd*.

 ## Words to Know

☐ Match pictures with the words *over*, *under*, *on*, and *around*.

 ## Let's Make Art!

☐ Draw a picture of yourself visiting with someone.

 ## Read for Meaning

☐ Find what happens in a story and tell why it happens.

Wrap Up Your Week Turn your paper over. Draw or write about what you did at school this week. What did you read? What did you learn about friendship?

Name _______________________   Date _______________________

My Work Plan

Put an ☒ next to the activities you complete.

 ## Listen Up!

☐ Find objects with the same beginning sound as in *fan* and end sound as in *leaf.*

 ## Let's Write!

☐ Write a caption.

 ## Word Work

☐ Find objects with names that begin or end with *Ff.*

 ## Words to Know

☐ Match pictures with words for feelings.

 ## Let's Make Art!

☐ Draw a picture that shows how an animal changes as it grows.

 ## Read for Meaning

☐ Tell what happens at the beginning, middle, and end of a story.

School + Home **Wrap Up Your Week** Turn your paper over. Draw or write about what you did at school this week. What did you read? What did you learn about how things we use today have changed?

My Work Plan

Put an ☒ next to the activities you complete.

Listen Up!

☐ Find objects with the same beginning sound as in *ox* and middle sound as in *block*.

Let's Write!

☐ Write a list.

Word Work

☐ Find objects that have short *Oo* in the beginning or middle of its name.

Words to Know

☐ Match pictures with the words *old*, *new*, *fast*, and *slow*.

Let's Make Art!

☐ Draw pictures of your school today and what it looked like long ago.

Read for Meaning

☐ Make a conclusion.

Wrap Up Your Week Turn your paper over. Draw or write about what you did at school this week. What did you read? What did you learn about why our feelings change?

My Work Plan

Put an **X** next to the activities you complete.

 ## Listen Up!

☐ Listen for sounds.

 ## Let's Write!

☐ Draw a picture and write about it.

 ## Word Work

☐ Find things that have short *Oo* in its name.

 ## Words to Know

☐ Match words with things that are hard, soft, smooth, and rough.

 ## Let's Make Art!

☐ Make animals with clay.

 ## Read for Meaning

☐ Tell what the book is mostly about.

School + Home

Wrap Up Your Week
Turn your paper over. Draw or write about what you did at school this week. What did you read? What did you learn about adventures?

My Work Plan

Put an ☒ next to the activities you complete.

 ## Listen Up!

☐ Listen for sounds.

 ## Let's Write!

☐ Show the steps taken in a story.

 ## Word Work

☐ Find things with names that begin with *Hh* like *helicopter*.

 ## Words to Know

☐ Draw pictures to show *before, after, beginning,* and *end.*

 ## Let's Make Art!

☐ Draw a picture of your favorite part of a story.

 ## Read for Meaning

☐ Tell what happens first, next, and last in a story.

School + Home **Wrap Up Your Week** Turn your paper over. Draw or write about what you did at school this week. What did you read? What did you learn about adventures you can have on a lucky day?

My Work Plan

Put an **☒** next to the activities you complete.

 ## Listen Up!
☐ Listen for sounds.

 ## Let's Write!
☐ Finish a poem.

 ## Word Work
☐ Find things with names that begin with *Ll* like *lamb*.

 ## Words to Know
☐ Match words with things that are *fuzzy*, *bumpy*, *furry*, and *sharp*.

 ## Let's Make Art!
☐ Make an animal's home.

 ## Read for Meaning
☐ Choose an event in the story and tell why it happens.

Wrap Up Your Week Turn your paper over. Draw or write about what you did at school this week. What did you read? What did you learn about adventures as animal can have?

My Work Plan

Put an ☒ next to the activities you complete.

 ## Listen Up!
☐ Listen for sounds.

 ## Let's Write!
☐ Write about what an animal looks like.

 ## Word Work
☐ Make words that begin with *cl*, *fl*, *pl*, or *sl*.

 ## Words to Know
☐ Match pictures with words for shapes.

 ## Let's Make Art!
☐ Make puppets.

 ## Read for Meaning
☐ Tell what happens first, next, and last in a story.

Wrap Up Your Week Turn your paper over. Draw or write about what you did at school this week. What did you read? What did you learn about adventures a little girl can have?

My Work Plan

Put an ☒ next to the activities you complete.

 ## Listen Up!
☐ Listen for sounds.

 ## Let's Write!
☐ Write a list.

 ## Word Work
☐ Find things with names that begin or end with *Gg* like *goose* and *rug*.

 ## Words to Know
☐ Draw pictures and match words to the pictures.

 ## Let's Make Art!
☐ Make an Antarctic scene.

 ## Read for Meaning
☐ Name and tell about a character.

Wrap Up Your Week
Turn your paper over. Draw or write about what you did at school this week. What did you read? What did you learn about having an adventure in Antarctica?

My Work Plan

Put an ☒ next to the activities you complete.

 ## Listen Up!

☐ Listen for sounds.

 ## Let's Write!

☐ Write a letter.

 ## Word Work

☐ Find things that have short *Ee* in the beginning or middle of its name.

 ## Words to Know

☐ Use a map to show *north*, *south*, *east*, and *west*.

 ## Let's Make Art!

☐ Make clouds.

 ## Read for Meaning

☐ Group things you do into two groups.

Wrap Up Your Week Turn your paper over. Draw or write about what you did at school this week. What did you read? What did you learn about adventures you can have in a city?

My Work Plan

Put an ☒ next to the activities you complete.

 ## Listen Up!

☐ Listen for sounds.

 ## Let's Write!

☐ Write a report about a city.

 ## Word Work

☐ Find things that have short *Ee* in the beginning or middle of its name.

 ## Words to Know

☐ Use words for time.

 ## Let's Make Art!

☐ Make a picture of a skyline.

 ## Read for Meaning

☐ Tell where a story takes place.

Wrap Up Your Week Turn your paper over. Draw or write about what you did at school this week. What did you read? What did you learn about transportation?

My Work Plan

Put an ☒ next to the activities you complete.

 ## Listen Up!

☐ Listen for sounds.

 ## Let's Write!

☐ Write a caption.

 ## Word Work

☐ Find things with names that begin with *Ww*.

 ## Words to Know

☐ Match pictures with words for the way people go places.

 ## Let's Make Art!

☐ Draw a picture of your favorite way to go places.

 ## Read for Meaning

☐ Tell what is real and what is make-believe.

School + Home **Wrap Up Your Week** Turn your paper over. Draw or write about what you did at school this week. What did you read? What did you learn about transportation in an emergency?

My Work Plan

Put an ☒ next to the activities you complete.

 ## Listen Up!

☐ Listen for sounds.

 ## Let's Write!

☐ Write a rhyme.

 ## Word Work

☐ Find things with names that end with *Xx*.

 ## Words to Know

☐ Match words with things that show *top*, *bottom*, *front*, and *back*.

 ## Let's Make Art!

☐ Draw a picture.

 ## Read for Meaning

☐ Choose an event in the story and tell why it happens.

 **Wrap Up Your Week** Turn your paper over. Draw or write about what you did at school this week. What did you read? What did you learn about transportation for jobs?

My Work Plan

Put an ☒ next to the activities you complete.

 ## Listen Up!
☐ Listen for sounds.

 ## Let's Write!
☐ Write a poem about transportation.

 ## Word Work
☐ Find things that have short *Uu* in the beginning or middle of its name.

 ## Words to Know
☐ Match pictures and words for jobs.

 ## Let's Make Art!
☐ Make a movie poster.

 ## Read for Meaning
☐ Tell how things are alike or different.

School + Home **Wrap Up Your Week** Turn your paper over. Draw or write about what you did at school this week. What did you read? What did you learn about trains?

My Work Plan

Put an ☒ next to the activities you complete.

 ## Listen Up!
☐ Listen for sounds.

 ## Let's Write!
☐ Make a letter.

 ## Word Work
☐ Build words with short *u*.

 ## Words to Know
☐ Match words for time with words on a calendar.

 ## Let's Make Art!
☐ Make a train car.

 ## Read for Meaning
☐ Tell what happens in the beginning, middle, and end of a story.

Wrap Up Your Week Turn your paper over. Draw or write about what you did at school this week. What did you read? What did you learn about how people travel?

My Work Plan

Put an ☒ next to the activities you complete.

 ## Listen Up!

☐ Listen for sounds.

 ## Let's Write!

☐ Write an invitation.

 ## Word Work

☐ Find things with names that begin with *Vv*.

 ## Words to Know

☐ Match words with pictures.

 ## Let's Make Art!

☐ Make a picture book that shows how people go places.

 ## Read for Meaning

☐ Tell what a book is mostly about.

School + Home **Wrap Up Your Week** Turn your paper over. Draw or write about what you did at school this week. What did you read? What did you learn about getting to school?

My Work Plan

Put an ☒ next to the activities you complete.

 ## Listen Up!
☐ Listen for sounds.

 ## Let's Write!
☐ Write a how-to report.

 ## Word Work
☐ Build words.

 ## Words to Know
☐ Match words with pictures.

 ## Let's Make Art!
☐ Make a collage.

 ## Read for Meaning
☐ Draw a conclusion.

School + Home **Wrap Up Your Week** Turn your paper over. Draw or write about what you did at school this week. What did you read? What did you learn about how schools are built?

My Work Plan

Put an ☒ next to the activities you complete.

 **Listen Up!**

☐ Listen for sounds.

 **Let's Write!**

☐ Write a list.

 **Word Work**

☐ Build words with short *a*.

 **Words to Know**

☐ Match words with pictures.

 **Let's Make Art!**

☐ Draw a plan for a building.

 **Read for Meaning**

☐ Tell how things are alike or different.

School + Home **Wrap Up Your Week** Turn your paper over. Draw or write about what you did at school this week. What did you read? What did you learn about building tools?

My Work Plan

Put an ☒ next to the activities you complete.

 **Listen Up!**

☐ Listen for sounds.

 **Let's Write!**

☐ Write a song about how people build.

 **Word Work**

☐ Build words with short *o*.

 **Words to Know**

☐ Match pictures with words for places.

 **Let's Make Art!**

☐ Make a beaver.

 **Read for Meaning**

☐ Name characters in a story and tell about them.

Wrap Up Your Week Turn your paper over. Draw or write about what you did at school this week. What did you read? What did you learn about beaver homes?

My Work Plan

Put an ☒ next to the activities you complete.

 ## Listen Up!

☐ Listen for sounds.

 ## Let's Write!

☐ Write a rhyme about a building.

 ## Word Work

☐ Build words with short *e*.

 ## Words to Know

☐ Match pictures with words.

 ## Let's Make Art!

☐ Make models of homes.

 ## Read for Meaning

☐ Tell what a book is mostly about.

Wrap Up Your Week Turn your paper over. Draw or write about what you did at school this week. What did you read? What did you learn about what friends can build together?

My Work Plan

Put an **☒** next to the activities you complete.

Listen Up!

☐ Listen for sounds.

Let's Write!

☐ Write a rhyme about people who build houses.

Word Work

☐ Build words with short *u*.

Words to Know

☐ Match pictures with words for places.

Let's Make Art!

☐ Paint a picture.

Read for Meaning

☐ Tell what happens in a story.

Wrap Up Your Week Turn your paper over. Draw or write about what you did at school this week. What did you read? What did you learn about who builds a house?

My Work Plan

Put an **X** next to the activities you complete.

 ## Listen Up!

☐ Listen for sounds.

 ## Let's Write!

☐ Write a poem about what people do to help build a house.

 ## Word Work

☐ Build words with short vowel sounds.

 ## Words to Know

☐ Use words for feelings.

 ## Let's Make Art!

☐ Draw pictures to show what people do to help build a house.

 ## Read for Meaning

☐ Tell where a story takes place.

Wrap Up Your Week Turn your paper over. Draw or write about what you did at school this week. What did you read? What did you learn about how ants build their nests?

My Work Plan

Put an ☒ next to the activities you complete.

 Listen Up!

 Read for Meaning

 Let's Make Art!

 Word Work

 Let's Write!

 Words to Know

Journal Writing

Draw an ☒ over the day of the week after you write in your journal.

Monday   Tuesday   Wednesday   Thursday   Friday

Practice Book

Circle the ☺ if you finished your work.

Circle the ☹ if you did not finish your work.

	Assignments	Did you finish?
Monday		☺ ☹
Tuesday		☺ ☹
Wednesday		☺ ☹
Thursday		☺ ☹
Friday		☺ ☹

Use this outline at each center to help children recall options if they finish the assigned activity.

What Can I Do?

1

2

3

4